Why Am I an Amphibian?

Greg Pyers

Chicago, Illinois

© 2006 Raintree
a division of Reed Elsevier Inc.
Chicago, Illinois

Customer Service 888-363-4266
Visit our website at www.raintreelibrary.com

For information, address the publisher:
Raintree, 100 N. LaSalle, Suite 1200, Chicago, IL 60602

Typeset in 21/30 pt Goudy Sans Book
Printed and bound in China by South China
Printing Company Ltd

10 09 08 07 06
10 9 8 7 6 5 4 3 2 1

Library of Congress Cataloging-in-Publication Data
Pyers, Greg.
  Why am I an amphibian? / Greg Pyers.
    p. cm. -- (Classifying animals)
  Includes bibliographical references.
  ISBN 1-4109-2018-6 (library binding-hardcover) --
  ISBN 1-4109-2025-9 (pbk.)
  1. Amphibians--Juvenile literature. I. Title.
  QL644.2.P95 2006
  597.8--dc22
                          2005012219

Acknowledgments
The author and publishers are grateful to the following for permission
to reproduce copyright material: APL/Corbis/© Joe McDonald: p. **6**,
/© David A. Northcott: p. **15**; Basco/gtphoto: p. **21**; Bradleyireland.
com: p. **9**; Tobias Eisenberg/imagequestmarine.com, pp: **12, 25**; Getty
Images/Image Bank, p. **14**, /Taxi: p. **17**; Francois Gohier: p. **18**; /Ardea
London Ltd.: p. **19**; © Brian Kenney: p. **24**; Alfredo Maiquez/Lonely
Planet Images: p. **8**; Photolibrary.com: p. **13**, /Peter Solness: p. **4**,/
Animals Animals: pp. **7, 23, 26–7**, /SPL, pp. **10, 22**; Brian Rogers/
Natural Visions: p. **16**; Dennis Sheridan/© David Liebman Nature
Stock: p. **20**.

Cover photograph of a red-eyed tree frog reproduced with permission
of APL/Corbis/© Joe McDonald.

Every effort has been made to contact copyright holders of any material
reproduced in this book. Any omissions will be rectified in subsequent
printings if notice is given to the publisher.

The paper used to print this book comes from sustainable resources.

Contents

Words that are printed in bold, **like this**, are explained in the glossary on page 31.

All Kinds of Animals

There are millions of different kinds of animals.
There are animals that have four legs, animals that
have more than 50 legs, and animals that have no
legs at all! There are animals that are long and thin,
animals that are round and wide, and animals that
can change their shape.

But have you noticed that, despite all these differences,
some animals are still rather similar to one another?

A toad has four legs and a round, wide body.

Sorting

In a carpentry shop, tools are sorted on different hooks so that the carpenter can find the right one. Animals that are similar to one another can also be sorted into groups. Sorting animals into groups helps us learn about them. This sorting is called **classification**.

This chart shows one way that we can sort animals into groups. Vertebrates are animals with backbones. Invertebrates are animals without backbones. Amphibians are vertebrates.

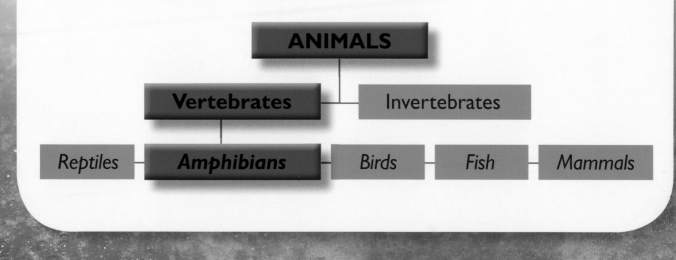

A Frog Is an Amphibian

Amphibians are one group of animals. There are about 5,740 **species**, or kinds, of amphibians. Frogs, salamanders, newts, and toads are amphibians. But lizards, otters, and seals are not. So, what makes an amphibian an amphibian? In this book, we will look closely at one amphibian, the red-eyed tree frog, to find out.

As you read through this book, you will see a ✔ next to important information that tells you what makes an amphibian an amphibian.

A red-eyed tree frog is bright green with blue and yellow sides, blue upper legs, orange-red feet, and red eyes.

Different frogs

Frogs are amphibians that have no tails. There are 4,740 species of frogs in the world. They live in many different places, called **habitats**. Many frogs live in **wetland** habitats, such as creeks and lakes. Some frogs live in deserts. The red-eyed tree frog lives in the rainforest of Central and South America.

Wet places

Amphibians are usually found in damp or wet places. Most amphibians prefer fresh water.

Tiger salamanders are often found in or near salty water in North America.

FAST FACT

The water-holding frog lives in the desert. It comes out of its hole in the soil only when rain falls.

A Frog's Body

Like all frogs, the red-eyed tree frog has a short, wide body. Other amphibians, such as newts, have long, thin bodies. Like most amphibians, the red-eyed tree frog has four legs. The red-eyed tree frog's back legs are very long. Long legs help this frog to climb. All tree frogs have sticky pads on their toes for gripping leaves and stems.

FAST FACT

Some amphibians, called caecilians (say "suh-silly-ans"), have no legs. These amphibians look like worms.

A red-eyed tree frog's toes work like suction cups.

Skin

The red-eyed tree frog has soft, moist skin. Toads are the only amphibians that have dry skin. ✔ Like all amphibians, a red-eyed tree frog has no hairs, feathers, or **scales** on its skin.

Many amphibians have skin that can taste horrible to a **predator**. The red-eyed tree frog's bright colors warn predators that it would not be tasty to eat. Many frogs and toads actually have poisonous skin. The cane toad has poison **glands** near its ears. A predator that eats a cane toad can be killed by this amphibian's poison.

A red-eyed tree frog can change the color of its skin to help it hide from predators.

9

Inside a Frog

Inside a red-eyed tree frog is a skeleton of bones, including a backbone. The backbone is actually made up of many small bones joined together.
✓ All amphibians have a skeleton and a backbone inside their body.

Body temperature

✓ Like all amphibians, a red-eyed tree frog's body is the same **temperature** as the air or water around it. Frogs that live in cool **habitats** usually have cool bodies. The red-eyed tree frog lives in a warm habitat, so its body is usually warm.

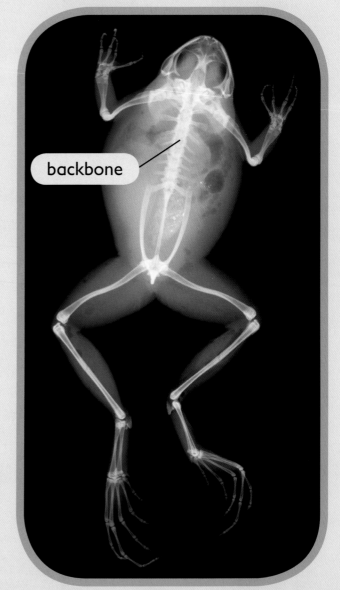

backbone

This X-ray picture shows the skeleton inside a frog's body.

10

Organs

There are **organs** inside a red-eyed tree frog. These include a heart, a liver, a stomach, and **lungs**. These organs all have important jobs to do.

FAST FACT

Most amphibians have lungs, but some salamanders have no lungs. These amphibians get all their oxygen through their skin.

Breathing

A red-eyed tree frog's lungs take in **oxygen** from the air. When a red-eyed tree frog breathes through its nostrils, air moves into its lungs. From there, oxygen passes into the blood. ✔ Like other amphibians, red-eyed tree frogs can also take in oxygen through their skin.

heart pumps blood around body

liver stores energy and helps break down food

stomach breaks down food

intestines pass **nutrients** into the blood

These are some of the organs inside a red-eyed tree frog.

lungs take in oxygen

Food

Red-eyed tree frogs are carnivorous. This means that they eat other animals. These other animals are the red-eyed tree frog's **prey**. When the frogs are small, their prey includes tiny insects, such as fruit flies. When they are fully grown, red-eyed tree frogs eat larger insects, such as grasshoppers. Sometimes they even eat other frogs.

A red-eyed tree frog pulls an insect into its mouth.

Hunting

A red-eyed tree frog hunts at night. It waits quietly on a branch. When an insect comes near, the frog shoots its tongue out at it. The tongue moves fast and its tip sticks to the insect. The frog then pulls its prey into its mouth. Some frogs do not have tongues. These frogs hunt for their prey under water.

Eating

A red-eyed tree frog swallows its food whole. It uses the teeth on the top of its mouth to grip its prey and keep it from escaping.

A red-eyed tree frog's eyes push down to help it swallow its food.

13

Senses

Like all amphibians, a red-eyed tree frog has senses to let it know what is going on around it.

Seeing and hearing

A red-eyed tree frog's large eyes give it an excellent sense of sight. Large eyes help the frog to see **prey** move in the darkness. A red-eyed tree frog has two ears, one on each side of its head. With these, the frog can hear other frogs calling.

A red-eyed tree frog's eyes give it a good all-around view.

Taste and smell

A red-eyed tree frog has taste buds on its tongue. If the tongue strikes prey that has a horrible taste, the frog will let it go. The red-eyed tree frog also has a sense of smell. It can use this sense to tell whether or not food is safe to eat.

Touch

You may have noticed that if you touch a frog, it will jump away. This shows that frogs have a good sense of touch.

A red-eyed tree frog smells with its nostrils.

nostril

Mating

In the rainy season, between October and March, male and female red-eyed tree frogs come together to **mate**.

Calling

At mating time, male red-eyed tree frogs begin calling from leaves low down in the rainforest. The males are calling female red-eyed tree frogs to come to them. They make a loud sound in their throats. The sound is kind of like a baby's rattle.

The sac under the male red-eyed tree frog's mouth fills with air as he calls. This makes the sound loud.

sac

Attracting a mate

Most male frogs and toads make sounds to attract females or to make females come to them. Different **species** make different sounds so that females know which male is which.

Getting ready to lay

When a female red-eyed tree frog reaches a male, the male climbs onto her back and holds on tight. The female holds onto the underside of a leaf with her sticky toe pads. Now, she is ready to lay her eggs.

The male red-eyed tree frog is smaller than the female.

FAST FACT

Male Eungella (say "yoon-jella") torrent frogs do not call. Instead, they wave their back legs to attract females.

17

Eggs

The eggs come out of the female red-eyed tree frog's **cloaca** (say "cloh-acka"), which is an opening in her bottom. It may take a day for the female to lay 50 eggs. The eggs stick to a leaf. ✔ Like all amphibian eggs, the red-eyed tree frog's eggs have no shell. This means that the eggs must stay moist, or they will dry out and die.

Red-eyed tree frog eggs have a jelly coating that keeps them moist.

18

Growing

As the female red-eyed tree frog lays her eggs, the male **fertilizes** them. An **embryo** begins to grow inside each egg. Each embryo will become a tadpole (see page 20).

Most **species** of frogs lay their eggs in water. But the female gastric-brooding frog swallows her eggs after the male has fertilized them. The embryos grow inside her stomach.

You can see red-eyed tree frog embryos growing inside the eggs.

19

Tadpoles

When a pair of red-eyed tree frogs **mate**, the female lays the eggs on a leaf that is hanging over water. All amphibians hatch from eggs. Red-eyed tree frog eggs hatch five days after they are laid. A tadpole, not a frog, comes out of each egg. The tadpoles fall into the water.

A tadpole is the first stage in a red-eyed tree frog's life. Only later will the tadpole become a frog.

All frogs begin their lives as tadpoles.

Two stages

✓ All amphibians have two stages in their lives. They have a **larva** stage and an **adult** stage. In frogs, the tadpole is the larva stage. The frog is the adult stage. Tadpoles are very different from frogs. They have **gills** for getting **oxygen** under water. Frogs have **lungs** that they use for breathing oxygen from the air.

FAST FACT

The word *amphibian* comes from two words: *amphi*, which means "both," and *bios*, which means "life." So, an amphibian is an animal that has an underwater life, which is usually followed by a life on land.

An adult red-eyed tree frog breathes air through its nostrils.

nostrils

The Life of a Tadpole

Tadpoles must live in water because they have **gills** instead of **lungs**. Without lungs, they cannot breathe air.

Food

Red-eyed tree frog tadpoles find food near the surface of the water. They eat algae, which are simple plants. They also eat tiny animals, such as the **larvae** of **aquatic insects**, and dead animals.

FAST FACT

Tadpoles of the turtle frog of Australia do not swim. Instead, they stay in their eggs until they become frogs.

These animals are mosquito larvae, or mosquito young. Red-eyed tree frog tadpoles eat mosquito larvae.

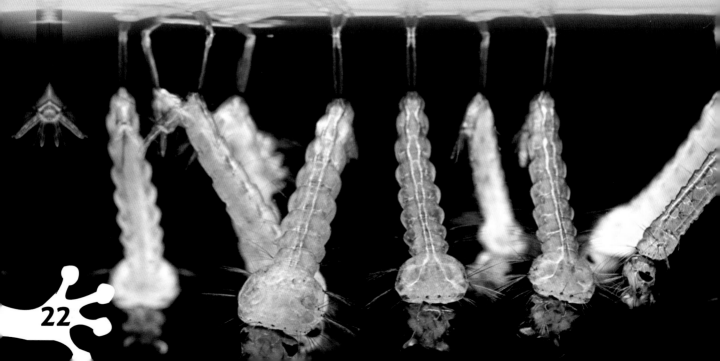

Dangers

Red-eyed tree frog tadpoles have many **predators**.
These are animals that kill and eat them. Birds and fish
eat many red-eyed tree frog tadpoles. Of all the tadpoles
that hatch from their eggs, only a few will survive long
enough to become frogs.

A heron hunts for red-eyed tree frog tadpoles to eat.

Becoming an Adult

The tadpoles become **adult** red-eyed tree frogs 75 to 80 days after hatching from their eggs. The process of turning from a tadpole into an adult frog is called **metamorphosis** (say "metta-morf-a-siss"). ✓ To become adults, all amphibians go through metamorphosis.

Changes in metamorphosis

As the red-eyed tree frog tadpole gets ready to change into a frog, two back legs begin to grow. Front legs grow two weeks later. The tadpole loses its **gills**. **Lungs** grow inside the tadpole's body.

With no gills, the tadpole (below, at this point called a froglet) cannot get **oxygen** from the water. It must breathe air.

FAST FACT

Some salamanders may keep their gills and stay in the **larva** stage for their entire lives. This means they never become adults. But they can still **mate**.

Leaving the water

The tadpole's head changes shape and its mouthparts are shed. There is a new mouth underneath. Now, it is a froglet with a tail. The froglet is a pale blue color. It leaves the water and moves into the damp grass or plants of the rainforest. Soon its tail disappears.

At last, the froglet becomes an adult red-eyed tree frog. It spends most of its time in the leaves alongside the pools and creeks of the rainforest. A red-eyed tree frog may live for five to eight years.

Red-eyed tree froglets' tails turn brown before they disappear.

Is It an Amphibian?

A red-eyed tree frog is an amphibian, because:

- ✔ It has a backbone
- ✔ It has two stages in its life: a **larva** stage with **gills**, then an **adult** stage with **lungs**
- ✔ Its body may be warm or cool, depending on its surroundings
- ✔ It hatches from an egg that has a very thin skin, instead of a shell
- ✔ It has no **scales**, hair, or feathers
- ✔ It can take in **oxygen** through its skin.

A red-eyed tree frog is an amphibian.

Test yourself: Mexican axolotls

Mexican axolotls (say "aks-uh-lottles") live in cold lakes high in the mountains. Their body **temperature** changes with the water temperature. They have gills, so they can get oxygen from the water. Their skin is smooth and slippery. Mexican axolotls have a backbone, four legs, and a long tail. If a Mexican axolotl is put into warm water, it will soon lose its gills, grow lungs, and begin living on land.

Is the Mexican axolotl an amphibian? You decide. (You will find the answer at the bottom of page 30.)

Mexican axolotls are also called Mexican walking fish, although they are not fish.

Animal Groups

This table shows the main features of the animals in each animal group.

Mammals	Birds	Reptiles
backbone	backbone	backbone
skeleton inside body	skeleton inside body	skeleton inside body
most have four limbs	four limbs	most have four limbs
breathe air with **lungs**	breathe air with lungs	breathe air with lungs
most have hair or fur	all have feathers	all have **scales**
most born live; three **species** hatch from eggs; females' bodies make milk to feed young	all hatch from eggs with hard shells	many hatch from eggs with leathery shells; many born live
steady, warm body **temperature**	steady, warm body temperature	changing body temperature

	Fish		Amphibians		Insects
	backbone		backbone		no backbone
	skeleton inside body		skeleton inside body		exoskeleton outside body
	most have fins		most have four limbs		six legs
	all have **gills**		gills during first stage; **adults** breathe air with lungs		breathe air, but have no lungs
	most have scales		no feathers, scales, or hair		many have some hair
	most hatch from eggs; some born live		all hatch from eggs without shells		many hatch from eggs; many born live
	changing body temperature		changing body temperature		changing body temperature

Find Out for Yourself

If there are **wetlands** in your local area, they are sure to have frogs living in them. The frogs may be hard to see, but you will know they are there when you hear their calls. Each **species** makes a different call. How many different calls can you hear?

For more information about frogs and other amphibians, you can read more books and look on the Internet.

More books to read

Harvey, Bev. *Amphibians*. Philadelphia: Chelsea House, 2002.

Kalman, Bobbie, and Jacqueline Langille. *What Is an Amphibian?* New York: Crabtree, 1999.

Savage, Stephen. *Amphibians: What's the Difference?* Chicago: Raintree, 2000.

Using the Internet

You can explore the Internet to find out more about amphibians. An adult can help you use a search engine. Type in a keyword such as *amphibians* or the name of a particular amphibian species.

Answer to "Test yourself" question:
A Mexican axolotl is an amphibian.

Glossary

adult   grown-up

aquatic insects   insects that live in water

classification   sorting things into groups

cloaca   opening in a female frog through which eggs are laid

embryo   early stage in the growth of a tadpole inside its egg

fertilize   make an embryo grow inside an egg

gills   organs that take in oxygen under water

gland   part of the body that makes a liquid, such as poison

habitat   place where an animal lives

larva (more than one are called larvae)   first stage in amphibian life. A tadpole is the larva of a frog.

lungs   organs that take in air

mate   come together to make new animals

metamorphosis   when a tadpole changes into a frog

nutrient   part of food that an animal needs to survive

organ   part of an animal's body that has a certain task or tasks

oxygen   gas that living things need to survive

predator   animal that kills and eats other animals

prey   animals that are eaten by other animals

scales   hard plates that cover skin

species   kind of animal

temperature   how warm or cold something is

wetland   lake, pond, stream, or swamp

Index

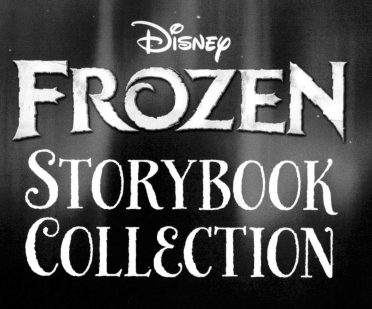

Disney
Frozen
Storybook
Collection

Disney PRESS

Los Angeles • New York

CONTENTS

THE KINGDOM OF ARENDELLE was a happy place. The king and queen had two young daughters, Anna and Elsa. But the family had a secret: Elsa could create ice and snow with her hands. One night, Anna convinced Elsa to turn the ballroom into a winter wonderland. As the sisters happily played together, Elsa accidentally lost control of her magic. An icy blast hit Anna in the head, and she fell to the floor, unconscious.

The king and queen rushed the girls to the trolls, mysterious healers who knew about magic. A wise troll named Grand Pabbie saved Anna by removing her memories of Elsa's magic. He explained that she was lucky to have been hit in the head, not in the heart.

The troll told the king and queen that Elsa's powers would only grow stronger. "Fear will be her enemy," he warned.

The king and queen knew they had to protect their daughter. To keep her magic a secret, they closed the kingdom's gates. The king gave Elsa gloves to contain her powers, but she was still afraid she might hurt someone. She even avoided Anna to keep her safe. Then, when Anna and Elsa were teenagers, their parents were lost at sea. The sisters had never felt more alone.

Elsa stayed inside, where she could hide her magic. But she could not keep the castle gates closed forever. On the day of her coronation, her subjects were invited inside to celebrate.

Elsa was nervous, but Anna was thrilled at the chance to meet new people! She had barely stepped outside the castle when she met Prince Hans of the Southern Isles. Anna was smitten with the handsome prince. The two instantly fell in love.

At the coronation ball, Prince Hans asked Anna to marry him. Anna said yes right away, and the couple went to ask Elsa for her blessing.

Elsa refused to bless the marriage. She couldn't let her younger sister marry a man she had just met!

Anna couldn't believe Elsa. "Why do you shut me out? What are you so afraid of?" she cried.

As Elsa fought with her sister, she lost control of her magic. Ice shot from her hands. Now all of Arendelle knew her secret. Panicked, Elsa fled into the mountains.

With her secret out, Elsa let her powers loose. A storm raged around her as she created an ice palace and even changed the way she looked. Below her, ice and snow covered Arendelle.

Anna felt awful! Leaving Hans in charge, she went after her sister.

As Anna trekked through the forest, she lost her horse. Luckily, she met an ice harvester named Kristoff and his reindeer, Sven. The two agreed to help her find Elsa.

High in the mountains, Anna and Kristoff came across a dazzling winter wonderland, where they met a living snowman.

"I'm Olaf," the snowman said.

Anna realized that Elsa must have created him. She asked Olaf to lead them to Elsa so she could bring back summer. Olaf loved the idea of summer and happily led them to Elsa's palace.

Inside, Anna told Elsa about Arendelle's winter storm.

"It's okay. You can just unfreeze it," she said.

But Elsa didn't know how to stop the snow and the winter storm. Frustrated, she cried out, "I can't!"

An icy blast shot across the room and hit Anna in the heart!

Kristoff rushed forward to help Anna. "I think we should go," he said.

At the base of the mountain, Kristoff noticed that Anna's hair was beginning to turn white. He knew his friends the trolls would be able to help her.

Grand Pabbie saw at once that Anna was hurt. "There is ice in your heart, put there by your sister," he said. "If not removed, to solid ice you will freeze, forever."

Grand Pabbie explained that only an act of true love could thaw a frozen heart. Anna knew Hans was her true love. Maybe a kiss from him would save her from freezing!

Anna, Kristoff, Sven, and Olaf raced back to Arendelle. Finding Prince Hans was their only hope.

But Hans was not in Arendelle. He had set out to look for Anna when her horse returned without her.

Hans and the search party arrived at Elsa's palace. The men attacked Elsa, and she defended herself. One of the men aimed a crossbow at Elsa! Hans pushed it aside, and the arrow hit a chandelier. It crashed to the ground, knocking Elsa out.

Hans and his men took the queen back to Arendelle and threw her in the castle's dungeon.

Outside the kingdom, Anna, Kristoff, Olaf, and Sven hurried down the mountain. Anna was getting weaker by the minute. Kristoff was worried about her. At the castle gates, he passed her to the royal servants. He was starting to realize that he cared deeply about Anna, but he knew her true love, Hans, could make her well again.

Anna found Hans in the library. She asked him to save her life with a kiss, but he refused! Hans had only been pretending to love Anna so he could take over Arendelle. He put out the room's fire and left Anna to freeze.

In the dungeon, all Elsa could think about was getting away from Arendelle. It was the only way to protect everyone, especially Anna, from her powers. Elsa became so upset that she froze the whole dungeon and escaped!

Alone in the library, Anna realized how reckless she had been. In trying to find love, she had doomed her sister and herself.

Just when Anna had given up all hope, Olaf burst through the door. The snowman lit a fire to warm her.

Anna worried that the fire would melt Olaf, but the snowman didn't care. "Some people are worth melting for," he said.

Just then, Olaf looked out the window. He saw Kristoff riding toward the castle on Sven and realized that Kristoff was Anna's true love!

Olaf helped Anna outside. Then she saw Hans about to strike Elsa with his sword! Anna threw herself in front of Elsa. Hans's sword came down just as Anna's body froze to solid ice.

Elsa wrapped her arms around her frozen sister. "Oh, Anna," she sobbed. Then something amazing happened: Anna began to thaw!

"An act of true love will thaw a frozen heart," Olaf said.

"Love!" Elsa cried, looking at Anna. "That's it!" Love was the key to her magic. She reversed the winter and brought back summer to Arendelle.

With summer restored, Arendelle returned to normal—but from then on, the castle gates were open for good. For the first time in a long while, Arendelle was a happy place again. And Queen Elsa and Princess Anna were the happiest of all, for they had found their way back to each other!

Childhood Times

IT WAS A BEAUTIFUL day in the kingdom of Arendelle. The Baron and Baroness of Snoob had just arrived for a visit. King Agnarr and Queen Iduna proudly welcomed their guests. If all went well, Arendelle would soon have a new trade partner.

Upstairs, Elsa and Anna stared at their breakfast in disbelief.

"We get chocolate just because we have visitors?" Anna asked.

"I suppose we *could* refuse to eat it," Elsa said, teasing her.

"No!" Anna chomped on her chocolate croissant. "Elsa, can we play with the magic?"

"We're supposed to stay in our rooms," Elsa said.

"Elsa, pleeeeease?" Anna begged.

"Okay!" Elsa agreed. "But we can't let them catch us!"

Together, the sisters snuck into the castle's grand hallway. The king and queen were still outside with their visitors, so Elsa raised her hands high in the air.

Whoosh! Glistening ice instantly covered the floors and railings.

"Whee!" Anna shouted as she slid across the floor.

"Anna, watch this!" Elsa said. With a wave of her arms, an icy rooster appeared—then a palm tree and a tiger!

Suddenly, the sisters heard the king and queen coming inside with the baron and baroness. They slipped away without being spotted!

The king and queen led the tour directly into the hallway. Anna and Elsa were gone, but the ice sculptures were still in place.

"Ah! I say!" the Baron of Snoob exclaimed. "These statues are absolutely extraordinary!"

His wife, the baroness, was less impressed.

Carefully, the girls crept to the kitchen. With a mischievous grin, Elsa made huge amounts of snow and ice. Soon the sisters were having a big snowball fight.

"See that pan?" Elsa shouted, pointing behind her. She hit it with a snowball. "Woo-hoo!"

The two girls were having so much fun that they almost didn't see the king and queen arriving with their royal visitors. Quickly, Anna and Elsa headed up the back staircase.

When the king and queen entered the kitchen, they were surprised to see all the ice. But the baron thought the snowballs were wonderful.

"Oh, my. This is just what we need on a warm summer's day!" he exclaimed. "You must try it, my dear!"

"*Harumph!*" The baroness stared at her icy snow cone.

"Ah, yes!" the king said, chuckling. "Ice is Arendelle's number one product!"

"Indeed! We harvest lots of ice from lakes up in the nearby mountains," the queen added, not mentioning that her daughter sometimes helped.

There was no stopping the girls! Anna and Elsa ran through the rest of the castle leaving a trail of ice and snow behind them. In the ballroom, Elsa made snowy hills. Both girls slid up into the air and then down again. Together they raced around the ballroom. They even made snow angels!

Suddenly, the girls heard the guests approaching.

"Uh-oh!" Elsa said, startled. "We'd better hide!"

Giggling, the girls raced back to their bedroom.

"That was close!" Anna chirped. "They almost saw us!"

Meanwhile, down in the ballroom, the king and queen gasped when they saw the snowy hills and the—

"Oof!" The baroness slipped and landed in a pile of snow.

"Oh, dear," the queen said. She and the king rushed to help their guests.

"Snow angels!" the baroness cried out. "I love snow angels. What a delightful surprise!"

"I say." The baron chuckled. "The kingdom of Arendelle stops at nothing to please its visitors!"

After the visitors had
gone to their guest rooms
for the evening, the king and
queen went to check on their
daughters.

They found the sisters in
Elsa's bed. Both appeared to
be sleeping soundly.

The queen smiled. She
knew the girls had been very
busy all day.

As their parents turned
away, a small smile appeared
on Anna's face. She listened for
the sound of the door closing
and then popped upright.

Anna looked at her big sister. "Elsa, do you want to play?" she asked.

"Anna, we can't! We're already going to be in a ton of trouble tomorrow," Elsa said.

Anna flopped back onto her pillow and sighed. "Still . . ."

"It was *so* worth it!" the girls said together.

A Royal Sleepover

"P SSSSST! ELSA?" ANNA NUDGED her sleeping sister. "Come on, wake up."

Elsa shifted, groggy. "Go back to bed, Anna. It's the middle of the night," she said.

"I can't sleep!" Anna flopped down on Elsa's bed.

Then Anna smiled slyly to herself. She knew how to get Elsa out of bed. "Wanna have a sleepover?"

This time, Elsa opened her eyes and grinned. That sounded like a lot of fun!

While Anna went to her room to find extra pillows and blankets, Elsa headed to the kitchen to get the ingredients for her famous honey cones. After all, a sleepover wasn't a sleepover without snacks!

When Elsa got back to her room, she found Anna digging through the closet. She was looking for something.

"Aha!" Anna cried. "I knew it was here!"

Anna held up an old worn book. Her parents had read it to the sisters every night when they were little.

"Let's see, we've got books, games, and this face cream Oaken gave me the last time I went to the trading post," Anna said. She opened the cream. "It looks kinda . . . goopy."

Elsa laughed. "Let's save that for later!"

Elsa looked around. It had been a long time since she'd had a sleepover.

"Sooo . . . what should we do first?" she asked.

Anna was ready. "How about we build a fort, like when we were kids?" she suggested.

Anna stacked pillows and blankets around the room, making lookouts and hidden caves. Meanwhile, Elsa created icy tunnels and snowy turrets.

"This is fun," Elsa said, putting the finishing touches on an icy archway. "I think we should add a—"

SMACK! Elsa felt something soft and feathery hit her back. She turned to see a fallen pillow and a giggling Anna.

"Oh, no you don't!" Elsa yelled, launching a snowball at her sister. Anna ducked, squealing in delight.

Before long, the room was covered in snow flurries and feathers. Anna was zooming down an icy slide on the fort when the sisters heard a knock at the door.

"Is it daytime already?" a familiar voice asked.

"Olaf!" Anna cried. The sisters welcomed their snowman friend inside.

Elsa explained that they were having a sleepover and invited Olaf to join them.

"A sleepover?" Olaf asked, excited. "Oh, I've always wanted to have one of those." He paused. "What's a sleepover?"

"We'll show you," Anna said. "Come on! I bet you'll be great at Pick-Up Sticks!"

Anna was right. Olaf was a natural at the fun game.

Anna was great at Work of Art. She guessed the drawing and sculpture every time!

Charades proved to be a bit more challenging. Olaf twisted his body this way and that, making frantic gestures and grinning widely. The sisters didn't know what the answer could be. Finally, Elsa had an idea.

"Olaf, are you acting out 'summer'?" she asked.

"Yes!" he cried. "You're good at this!"

Elsa laughed. "Maybe it's time to do something else," she said. "How about a scary story?"

Anna went first, using her spookiest, most dramatic voice. She even held a candle up to her face, casting eerie shadows on the wall behind her. "According to legend, the Hairy Hooligan only comes out on nights like these, looking for his next victim," she said.

"How do you know when the Hairy Hooligan is around?" Olaf asked.

"He lets out a low moan," Anna answered.

"*OOOOOOOHHHHH.*" A sad whine echoed through the room.

"Wow. That's really scary, Anna," Olaf said, impressed.

"Uh . . ." Anna blinked. "That wasn't me."

"*OOOOOOOOOHHHHH!*" The cry sounded like it was coming from outside the castle.

A sudden noise made them all jump. Elsa, Anna, and Olaf ran to the window. A shadowy figure was walking toward them!

"Stay here," Elsa said, running down the hall. But Anna and Olaf followed. They couldn't let Elsa face the Hairy Hooligan alone!

Elsa opened the castle door, and the friends peered into the darkness. Olaf held Anna's hand, bracing himself for the Hairy Hooligan's pointed teeth and sharp claws.

But it wasn't a monster after all. It was Sven!

"Sven!" Elsa called out. "What's the matter?"

Anna took one look at the reindeer and guessed what was going on. "You couldn't sleep, could you, Sven?" She patted him gently on the nose. "I bet Kristoff is snoring and keeping you awake. The trolls said his snores are loud enough to start an avalanche!"

Sven nodded.

"You should come to our sleepover!" Olaf said. "From what I can tell, there's very little sleeping involved."

Soon the group was happily settled in Elsa's room.

Anna got Sven and Olaf to try the face cream from Oaken, and they all laughed as the goop slid down their chins. "How about another story?" Elsa suggested, holding up a book.

"Excellent!" Anna agreed. She fluffed some pillows, and she, Olaf, and Sven got comfortable as Elsa began reading.

A little while later, Elsa finished the story. She looked around, hearing the sounds of heavy breathing around her. The rest of the slumber party had fallen asleep!

Smiling, Elsa put down the book. She gently tucked in Anna, Olaf, and Sven and climbed into bed. Then, with one last look at Anna and her friends, Elsa, too, drifted off to sleep.

OAKEN'S INVENTION

HIGH IN THE MOUNTAINS above Arendelle was a special store—Wandering Oaken's Trading Post and Sauna. Oaken loved his store. He loved helping his customers and he loved his sauna. But most of all, he loved inventing new things that people might enjoy.

The only thing Oaken loved more than inventing things was spending time with his family. The next day was the biannual Oaken family reunion. His family would be coming from all over the different parts of Arendelle to visit his shop! Oaken was really excited to see everyone.

The Oaken family reunion was always fun. Oaken's aunts and uncles gobbled up lutefisk and lingonberry pie while his cousins played Reindeer Ringtoss and made snow angels. The whole family enjoyed participating in the Polar Plunge, followed by a nice warm steam in Oaken's sauna.

But the best part of the reunion was the Creator's Contest, when Oaken's family members shared the wonderful contraptions they had invented since the last family reunion. It was always full of surprises.

The Creator's Contest was usually Oaken's favorite family tradition, but this year he had a problem. He didn't have a new invention to show! Oaken felt bad. He didn't want to let his family down.

The shopkeeper was so lost in thought that he didn't even notice when the shop's bell jangled and Kristoff walked in.

Oaken didn't call out his usual greeting, so Kristoff tried it himself. "Hoo-hoo!" he called. "Ice delivery!"

Startled, Oaken looked up. "Hoo-hoo," he said gloomily.

"What's wrong, Oaken?" Kristoff asked.

Oaken sighed. "I haven't invented anything for my family's Creator's Contest tomorrow."

"Inventing can be a tough business," Kristoff said. "But sometimes inspiration can come from the most unexpected places."

Oaken nodded, but he wasn't sure he agreed with the ice harvester.

"Don't worry about it, Oaken," Kristoff said as he walked toward the door. "I'm sure you'll think of something!"

After Kristoff left, Oaken
tried to think of an
invention. But none
of his ideas seemed
special enough
for the Creator's
Contest. Finally, he
decided to take a
break in his sauna. A
hot steam might clear
his mind and help him think.

As Oaken made his way toward the
sauna, he tripped over the stack of ice blocks Kristoff had delivered. One of
the blocks slid toward a clearing in the trees.

As it came to rest, the edges of the ice started to glow a soft silver.
Curious, Oaken walked to the ice block.

As he approached the block, Oaken saw the colors from the northern lights glinting through the ice, causing it to glow. Suddenly, Oaken had an idea. He knew exactly what to invent for the Creator's Contest. Oaken picked up the ice and raced back to his shop. He didn't have a moment to waste!

The next day, Oaken's family arrived. Everyone was happy to see one another. "Hoo-hoo!" each one called out in greeting. The adults ate krumkake while the children raced their sleds. Finally, after a day of games and activities, it was time for the Creator's Contest. The family gathered around to see what wonderful new inventions their relatives had come up with.

Grandma Hedda held
up a sweater that had
earmuffs attached to the
neck with a string.

Cousin Agathe played
her newest composition on
her Hardanger fiddle. Some
of the family appreciated
that more than others.

At long last, it was Oaken's turn.

"Follow me, family," he sang out.

Excited, Oaken's family followed him. They wondered what he could possibly have made.

"I hope whatever it is will be as good as the shoes for walking on snow," Aunt Klara said.

Oaken led his family into the clearing. Standing by itself in the middle of the trees was an enormous block of ice.

"That's a nice big block of ice ya got there, Oaken," Cousin Lars said. "But what does it do?"

"You'll see," Oaken said, putting out the fire in his lantern. Everything went black. Oaken's family looked around, confused.

Just then, the northern lights appeared in the sky! As their light hit the block of ice, bright bursts of color erupted everywhere, sparkling on the trees, against the snow, and across the faces of the astonished Oaken clan.

Oaken beamed proudly.

"It's a lantern for the temporary capturing of polar lights," he explained, pointing to the sky. "For the celebrating of special moments, like Oaken family reunions."

Oaken's family was astonished. It was beautiful! Everyone agreed that Oaken had the best invention. He was the winner of the Creator's Contest. Oaken was delighted to have won, but he had realized something more important. Spending time with his family was the best prize of all!

ON THE TRAIL

AS THE SUN SLIPPED behind the mountain, Little Rock roused the group. "It's wake-up time! We have to find Grand Pabbie." He reminded them that there were only two days left of autumn. Little Rock was determined to earn his tracking crystal and participate in the crystal ceremony with the other level-one trolls.

With everyone finally on their feet, Little Rock confidently marched down the trail with the group following behind.

"I'm going to find clues," Little Rock announced, "and leave no shrub unturned." He scanned the area and froze when something caught his eye.

"Grand Pabbie must have gone this way," he said, holding up a broken-off branch.

Olaf rushed over. "Arm!" he shouted. "I wondered where I left you."

At everyone's puzzled expressions, he explained he had lost it when he tried to shoo a bug out of his face.

Kristoff noticed Little Rock's look of disappointment and reminded him that everyone makes mistakes. "And imagine how Olaf would have felt if he left his arm up on the mountain forever."

Little Rock brightened. "Glad I could help."

Then something in the distance caught Little Rock's eye. He raced ahead to check it out.

"An important clue!" he exclaimed.

Little Rock held up a clumpy piece of bright-green moss. "From Grand Pabbie's cloak," he said. "I'd know it anywhere."

"Oooh! I have a clue, too," said Olaf, holding up his moss-covered foot.

Elsa pointed out thick patches of the soft green plant scattered all over. "It's possible that it's just . . . moss."

Little Rock looked around and saw that Elsa was right. He sighed. "This isn't from Grand Pabbie's cloak."

As they walked farther up the mountain, snow appeared on the path. Anna and Kristoff discovered what they thought were troll footprints just off the trail. They called Little Rock over, but he was busy inspecting some other prints he had found.

"I think I have a real clue over here!" he shouted.

"I feel like I'm becoming a better tracker," Little Rock said as he followed the tracks to . . . Sven! Little Rock was starting to feel discouraged.

It took Anna a while to convince Little Rock to cheer up and check out the tracks she and Kristoff had found.

"Those are Grand Pabbie's footprints!" he declared.

They followed the prints, higher and higher up the mountain. But when they made it to the very top, the tracks stopped. Then they looked up and saw a dark cloud in the sky getting bigger by the second, and it started to snow.

When the snow began to fall harder, Elsa got to work.
She waved her arms and a beautiful ice shelter
appeared near them. They hurried to gather inside the
magical ice dome.

"We may be here for a little while," said Kristoff as he settled down in the cozy shelter.

"How about a story?" said Little Rock. "Anyone have one to share?"

Olaf raised his twig arms excitedly. "This storm reminds me of a story I know. And it's about the northern lights. On a very cold, very snowy night, Elsa built me with her magic. I remember saying, 'I'm Olaf and I like warm hugs.'

"Then I went exploring. And I got going so fast that I tumbled all over the place. I lost my head and my butt and my middle! Everything was swirling around and around. I loved it! And some of my parts collected things along the way."

"What about your nose?" asked Little Rock.

"That came later. From Anna," Olaf said. "So anyway, when I got to the bottom, I had to figure out where everything went."

"And when I was putting my final part in the right place, bright lights suddenly appeared in the sky."

"The northern lights!" cried Little Rock.

All at once they noticed the wind had stopped. Olaf looked outside the shelter and saw that the storm had passed.

Little Rock immediately started digging. "I'm trying to uncover Grand Pabbie's footprints," he explained.

"Maybe Grand Pabbie went down the mountain," offered Elsa. They all gazed over the steep drop, wondering how they could get down.

Little Rock grinned when he had an idea. "Remember your story, Olaf?

Maybe we could do that!"

Olaf nodded. Then he leapt over the side and began tumbling down.

Little Rock rolled into a ball and followed him!

Then Elsa, Anna, and Kristoff dove off the ledge. They laughed as they

slid, slipped, and rolled, racing one another down the mountain!

When they reached the bottom, Little Rock thanked Olaf for giving him the idea with his story. "Olaf," he said, "you deserve to carry my snow crystal."

Kristoff smiled proudly at Little Rock. "That was very observant of you, Little Rock," he said. "You realized that Olaf's story was an effective way to get down the steep mountain."

Little Rock grinned. He knew he was ready for whatever came next.

What Do You Get a Reindeer Who Has Everything?

OLAF LOVED TO EXPLORE Arendelle on beautiful sunny days. He danced through the meadow outside the palace gates, stopping only to smell and pick flowers. Elsa, Kristoff, and Anna trailed behind him, enjoying the sunshine and chattering happily among themselves.

Elsewhere in the meadow, Sven pranced back and forth, chasing butterflies. All in all, it was the perfect day to be outside!

Suddenly, Anna stopped walking. She turned to Kristoff, Elsa, and Olaf.

"I can't wait to give Sven his birthday present—antler polish," she said.

"What did you guys get him?"

"I got him a new harness," Elsa replied. "And a carrot cake!"

"I bought him some imported lichens," Kristoff said.

"It's Sven's birthday?" Olaf asked. "But I didn't get him anything."

"Don't worry, Olaf," Kristoff said. "It's actually tomorrow. Or maybe it's next week?" He shrugged. "Anyway, we always celebrated around this time of year with the trolls. They weren't big on exact dates!"

"Well, *we're* celebrating tomorrow," Anna said.

Later, at the castle, Olaf tried to think of a good birthday present for Sven. His friends had gotten Sven great gifts. Olaf wanted to give his reindeer friend something special, too.

He looked around the castle. "Ooh, a book!" he said. "Or a vase. Or a quill and some ink!"

Everything Olaf saw seemed perfect. How was he going to choose just one gift?

Olaf was looking at a large pile of gifts when Elsa appeared.

"Is everything okay, Olaf?" she asked.

"I don't know what to get Sven for his birthday," Olaf explained.

Elsa thought for a minute. "Well," she said, "sometimes the best gift is something that means a lot to you."

Olaf beamed at Elsa. She was so smart. No wonder she was queen! That was the best idea he'd heard all day.

Olaf went outside to think. As he stepped outside, his snow flurry appeared. Suddenly, Olaf knew *exactly* what to get Sven!

First Olaf needed a box. He dug through the castle closets until he found one that was just the right size.

Next Olaf went to the stables. He carefully packed the box full of the freshest hay. He wanted to make sure his gift for Sven had plenty of padding!

Finally, everything was ready. Olaf held out his hand and caught one of the snowflakes from his flurry.

"Hello, snowflake," Olaf said. "Sven is going to love you, just like I do."

Olaf was sure Sven would appreciate the cold snowflake on such a hot day. He carefully placed the snowflake on top of the bed of hay. Then he closed the box and tied a ribbon around it.

"Nice and snug!" he said. "See you soon, little snowflake!"

The next day was Sven's
party. Kristoff hung balloons
and streamers while Anna
set up the party games.

Soon the friends were
bobbing for carrots and playing
pin the tail on the reindeer.

"Who wants cake?" Elsa
asked, revealing a homemade
carrot cake, complete with
candles shaped like carrots
and frosting that looked like
snow!

The friends sang "Happy
Birthday" to Sven, and he
blew out the candles.

Olaf had been waiting all day to give Sven his gift. Finally, he couldn't wait any longer.

"Time for presents, Sven!" he said, eagerly grabbing his box for the reindeer. Everyone agreed.

Sven was delighted by the new harness from Elsa. He was thrilled with his antler polish from Anna. And he loved the imported lichens from Kristoff. Finally, Olaf handed Sven his gift.

Sven pulled the ribbon off the box, nudged the lid aside, and . . .

The snowflake was gone! Olaf looked around, confused. He didn't understand what could have happened to it.

"Wow, Olaf!" Kristoff said. "You found Sven the best gift of all."

"Huh?" Olaf said, looking at the reindeer. Sven was nose-deep in the box, munching happily.

PRINCESS ANNA LOOKED AROUND the courtyard. "It's the perfect day for the annual ice-carving contest," she told her sister, Queen Elsa. "Cold and clear and bright."

Elsa smiled. She had loved this contest when she was younger. Now that the castle gates were open again, she was thrilled to bring back the tradition. Ice harvesters had dragged large blocks of ice into the castle courtyard so the contestants could carve their creations. And from the crowd, it seemed as if almost everyone in Arendelle was taking part in the contest.

Olaf ran up to the sisters. The little snowman tugged on Anna's dress. "Come on, Anna," he said. "Let's find our ice!"

"Okay," Anna said with a laugh. "See you later, Elsa!"

"Good luck," Elsa called as Olaf took Anna by the hand. They picked up some carving tools and made their way to their block of ice.

Nearby, Kristoff and Sven were admiring their own block of ice.

"I know this is my first time *sculpting* ice," Kristoff said, "but I've been cutting blocks of ice since I was a kid. How hard could it be?"

Sven nodded.

"We work with ice every day," Kristoff said. "We know the secrets of the ice. I know we'll make a great sculpture!"

Just then, Elsa clapped her hands.

"Good morning, everyone!" she said. "Welcome to the ice-carving contest!"

The crowd cheered.

"The rules are simple," Elsa said. "Carvers may either work alone or in teams of two. Each team will have until the sun sets to finish their sculpture. Then I will choose the winners. You may now begin. Good luck, everyone!"

As the carvers took their places, Anna saw Kristoff and Sven. Their block of ice was right next to hers and Olaf's!

"I didn't know you were entering the contest," she said to Kristoff.

"I didn't know you were entering, either," Kristoff replied.

"I guess I should have known," Anna said with a smile. "After all, ice is your life."

Kristoff laughed. He couldn't disagree with that!

Anna held out her hand. "Good luck," she said.

"May the best artist win!" Kristoff replied.

Anna and Olaf picked up their tools and together began chipping away at the ice. Anna leaned back and struck the ice with her chisel.

"Whoa! That was so much fun!" Anna said, taking another swing at the ice.

Olaf giggled with delight as he took a chip out of the block with his chisel. "This *is* fun! I wonder what it is we're making!"

"I guess we'll find out," Anna shouted as she happily hammered away at their block, sending ice chips spraying into the air all around them.

Meanwhile, Kristoff and Sven carefully searched their block of ice for lines and cracks. Kristoff put his ear to the ice and closed his eyes.

"Okay, Sven. Now I know where the ice will break!" Kristoff said finally.

Nearby, Anna saw Kristoff and Sven carefully start to carve their ice. She stopped and looked down at her own block of ice. She and Olaf had been having so much fun chipping away that their ice didn't look like anything. Maybe Kristoff had the right idea.

Anna and Olaf stopped carving and put down their tools. Kneeling, Anna tried to listen to the ice.

"What's it saying, Anna?" Olaf asked.

"I don't hear anything," Anna said. But then she noticed all the small lines and cracks in the ice. Now she knew where the ice would break! The friends picked up their tools and merrily started chipping away again.

The pair's laughter caught Kristoff's attention. Although their sculpture looked a little funny, Anna and Olaf seemed to be having a good time.

Kristoff looked at Sven and their block of ice. They had barely made a dent in it.

"Maybe we don't need to be so careful," Kristoff told Sven. "And I think I know just what we should carve."

He whispered something in Sven's ear. The reindeer smiled. Then the two of them got back to work. Kristoff used his chisel, and Sven used the sharp points of his antlers. Soon they were laughing, too.

As the hours ticked by, all the teams worked hard on their sculptures. Soon many of the sculptures began to take shape. One team was carving a dolphin. Another was working on a sculpture of an ocean bird. Kristoff and Sven slowly worked on their creation, while Anna and Olaf kept chipping away as quickly as they could.

Anna couldn't believe how much fun she was having. Ice carving might be her new hobby!

Finally, Elsa's voice rang out through the courtyard.

"The sun is setting!" she said. "It's time for the judging to begin."

Elsa walked up and down the rows, looking at each team's carving. One of the ice harvesters had carved a cute polar bear cub.

"That's wonderful!" said Elsa.

Then she looked at Kristoff and Sven's sculpture. She smiled.

"It looks like Sven! What a good idea," she said. "It's too bad you weren't able to finish."

Next Elsa moved to Anna and Olaf's sculpture.

"Well, you finished your sculpture," she said. "But what is it?"

"Can't you tell?" Olaf asked. "It's an ice man!"

"Oh, of course," Elsa said politely to Anna and Olaf. "It's . . . it's wonderful!"

Elsa moved from team to team, looking at the rest of the sculptures. She saw a fish, a dolphin, and a seagull. She saw a cat, a swan, and a sailing ship. There were many beautiful sculptures to choose from. It was going to be hard for Elsa to pick just one winner.

Finally, she stopped at Olina and Kai's sculpture. They had carved the castle.

Elsa couldn't believe her eyes. "It's beautiful!" she cried. "Just look at this detail. You've carved every window, every tower, and every brick!"

Elsa turned to the crowd. "Olina and Kai are the winners!" she announced, placing a ribbon on their sculpture.

As the crowd erupted into applause, Olina and Kai smiled proudly.

"You know," Kristoff told Anna, "I bet we could make something great if we had the right team."

Anna grinned. "Maybe next time we all can work together," she said. "You can listen to the ice."

"And you can make sure Sven and I don't get too serious," Kristoff added.

The two friends shook hands. They couldn't wait until the next contest!

The Midsummer Parade

IT WAS A BEAUTIFUL summer day. The breeze was soft, the sun was warm, and birds were singing happily. Elsa and Anna were picking wildflowers in a field not far from town.

"I can't believe it'll be midsummer soon," Anna said, looking around the lush green meadow.

Elsa grinned. "I love midsummer," she said. "Remember when we were kids and I used to lead—"

"The midsummer parade!" Anna interrupted, finishing her sister's sentence. The midsummer parade was one of her happiest childhood memories.

"I *loved* that parade," Anna told her sister. "You always looked so fancy, riding at the head of it."

"On that chubby little pony," Elsa said with a chuckle. "Mister Waffles."

"We haven't had a midsummer parade since we were little kids," Anna said.

Elsa nodded. "Now that the gates are open, we should have it again. Starting this year!"

Anna clapped her hands. "You'll look so great at the head of the parade," she told her sister.

Elsa grinned. "Not me. *You!* I hereby declare you Midsummer Princess."

Anna, Elsa, and their friends started planning the parade the very next day.

"Marching band?" Elsa said.

"Already rehearsing," Kristoff said.

"Flowers?" Anna asked.

"I've been collecting them all—*achoo!*—week!" Olaf said, sniffling.

Anna consulted the parade planning checklist. "Next up, clothing!"

Anna and
Elsa went to
search the royal
wardrobe.

"How about
this?" Anna
asked, putting a
silly hat on Elsa.

Elsa giggled
and held up
some boots.

"These are definitely you," she told Anna.

The sisters picked wilder and wilder outfits for each other. Soon they
were laughing so hard they could hardly stand.

"Okay, it's time to get serious," Elsa said. "You need something special
to wear to the parade!"

With a little help from Anna's friends, the parade was shaping up beautifully. It was going to be exactly like when Anna and Elsa were kids! Well . . . almost exactly.

"I don't think you can ride Mister Waffles in the parade," Elsa told Anna. "You're bigger than he is now. Besides, I'm pretty sure he's retired."

"Then I'll have to find a new horse!" Anna said. "The best horse in all of Arendelle."

Anna and Olaf headed to the stable to find the right horse. "What about that one?" Anna asked the head groom, pointing at an elegant mare.

"She's so pretty!" Olaf sighed.

"This is Lady Crystalbrook Shinytoes the Fourth," the head groom said.

Lady Crystalbrook Shinytoes the Fourth stepped toward Anna . . . and tripped over her own feet. She fell right into the pond!

"Oh, dear," Anna said.

"How about him?" Olaf asked, pointing at a big strong horse. "What's his name?"

The groom cleared his throat. "Dauntless."

"Hello, Dauntless," Anna said. As she stepped forward to pet the horse, a leaf fluttered by in the wind. When Dauntless saw the leaf, his eyes widened. With a loud, frightened whinny, he turned and ran away as fast as he could.

"I do *not* think you should ride *him*," Olaf said.

Anna thought the third horse looked very promising . . .

until he tried to eat Olaf's nose!

"Hey!" Olaf giggled. "That tickles!"

Hours later, Anna was at her wits' end. They had met every horse, but they hadn't found the right one. "I don't know what to do," she said. "Maybe we should just cancel the parade."

"Cancel the parade?"

Anna and Olaf looked up to find Kristoff approaching. "Why would you do that?" he asked.

"I can't find the right horse to lead the parade," Anna said.

"Hmmm," Kristoff said. "I think I know just the fellow for the job."

"You do?" Olaf said. "Who's the horse?"

"Well . . ." Kristoff said, "he isn't exactly a *horse*."

"Sven," Kristoff said, slinging his arm around the reindeer's shoulders, "how would you like to lead the parade?"

"Gee whiz," Kristoff said in Sven's voice, speaking for his friend, "I'd be delighted!" And Sven *did* look delighted.

"Oh," Anna said, clasping her hands, "Sven is *perfect*! He's loyal, and brave, and smart!"

"And handsome," Kristoff added in his Sven voice.

"And handsome," Anna agreed. She kissed Sven's nose.

Anna looked at the checklist. "Band, flowers, Sven . . . I think everything's ready," she said.

Olaf jumped up and down in excitement. "It's parade time!" he cried.

The birds sang, the band played, and the people of Arendelle cheered as the parade wound its way through town. Anna was so happy she couldn't stop smiling.

ONE AFTERNOON, ANNA AND Olaf were in the royal library when Olaf spied a large pink book.

"Ooh! I like this one!" Olaf said. "Wait. What's it about?"

Anna read the title aloud: "'How to Find a Ghost.'"

"I love ghosts!" Olaf announced. "What's a ghost?"

"Well, it's . . ." Anna smiled and put her book down. "I have an idea. Follow me!"

Minutes later, Anna and Olaf burst into Elsa's office.

"Elsa!" Anna said. "Olaf wants to learn about ghosts, and I think—"

"We should have an indoor campout and go looking for one!" Elsa finished.

"Exactly!" Anna said.

Hours later, Elsa gathered some snacks from the kitchen, and Anna grabbed lots of pillows and blankets from their bedrooms. Then they met Olaf and began to look for a dark, spooky room they could use.

They ended up in an old, unused portion of the castle.

"I can't wait to learn about ghosts!" Olaf said.

"Let's make a fire and roast marshmallows first," Anna said.

"Ooh, I just love warm fireplaces!" Olaf declared.

"Is it time to learn about ghosts?" Olaf asked.

"Yes," Anna said. "You go first, Elsa!"

Elsa laid the book on her lap and began to read. "'Long ago, on a dark night in Arendelle . . .'" she whispered. She continued her story as Olaf listened, wide-eyed.

A while later, Elsa heard
Anna snort. She had fallen asleep.

"Well, Olaf, I guess my ghost story made Anna pretty tired. Come to think of it, I'm tired, too!" Elsa said as she yawned and snuggled down under her blanket. "Maybe we'll find a ghost tomorrow."

"I'd like to meet a ghost," Olaf said before blowing out the candles.

Soon both sisters were sound asleep.

But Olaf couldn't rest. He wanted to meet a ghost as soon as possible! As he looked at the pictures in the book, he remembered something Elsa had read to him. Apparently, ghosts got lonely and wandered around at night.

"Sometimes I get lonely and wander around at night, too!" Olaf said. "Maybe the ghost and I could wander together!"

As Olaf walked down the hallway, he noticed how dark it was. The only light came from the windows! He looked right, and he looked left. He looked up and down. But he didn't see any ghosts.

"Hello?" Olaf said. "Ghost? I'm here to be your friend!"

But nobody answered.

Olaf turned a dark corner at the end of a hallway, and then—

THUNK!

THUMP!

THUMP-THUMP-THUMP.

THUMP.

Olaf tumbled down a staircase!

THUMP!

Anna and Elsa woke with a start.

"What was that?" they asked in unison. Then, "I don't know!" they exclaimed quietly.

"And where is Olaf?" Anna asked.

Elsa lit some candles, and they wandered into the hallway.

"Oooh!" came a little voice from the bottom of the staircase.

Anna gasped. "That sounded like—"

"A ghost?" Elsa said.

They crept down, down, down the stairs.

"Hello? Are you there, Sir Ghost?" Elsa said.

"We want to be your friends!" Anna added.

"Oh-oh-oh! I want to be friends, too!" the ghost said.

Anna and Elsa stopped short.

"Are you ghosts?" the ghost asked.

"Wait," said Anna suspiciously.

"Do you like warm hugs? I do!" the ghost said.

"Yes," said Elsa, "we do like warm hugs. Are you—"

"Olaf?" Anna asked.

Elsa quickly pulled off the sheet.

"Oh! I can see again!" Olaf exclaimed. "Thank you, ghost that looks just like Elsa!"

"I *am* Elsa!" she replied with a laugh.

"Oh, okay," said Olaf. Then he pointed to Anna. "And you are . . . ?"

"Anna," said Anna.

"Olaf, you made this our best ghost hunt ever!" said Anna.

"But I didn't find any ghosts," Olaf replied.

"Well, maybe you didn't, but you became the best ghostlike snowman we've ever seen!" Elsa declared.

BULDA'S CRYSTAL

KRISTOFF AND SVEN WERE visiting the trolls. They had come to help them harvest mushrooms while Grand Pabbie was away. Now, after a long day, they were relaxing by the campfire with Bulda and the other trolls.

As the fire began to fade, one of Bulda's crystals started to flicker. "Oh, no!" she said, surprised. "My crystal is going dark."

"Don't worry," said Kristoff. "You have plenty of others."

"Yes, but this is my favorite," Bulda said. "Grand Pabbie gave it to me when you first came to live with us."

Bulda looked down at her crystal. "When this type of crystal goes dark, it must be recharged by the next time the northern lights fade from the sky or its magical glow will be lost. Grand Pabbie would know how to do it, but he's not here."

Kristoff looked at Bulda. She had given him and Sven a home. He was grateful to her for so much, and he hated to see her disappointed. "Sven and I will fix your crystal," he said.

At sunrise, Kristoff and Sven set off for Arendelle. They found Anna, Elsa, and Olaf in the library.

"There's a book about crystals in here somewhere," Elsa suggested, grabbing a large dusty book. Quickly, she scanned the pages. "This says that troll crystals can be reenergized 'where lights wake the sky, where sky touches the earth, and where waters run long.'"

"Lights that wake up the sky could be the northern lights," Kristoff said. "And 'where sky touches the earth' could be a mountaintop."

"There's a long, narrow fjord by Opplading Mountain," Anna said. "I bet that's 'where waters run long'!"

Opplading Mountain was a full day's journey from Arendelle. The friends quickly packed food, blankets, and a map and set out on their quest.

The group had been hiking all morning when they arrived at the top of a steep cliff. Kristoff looked over the side, searching for a trail to follow.

"According to the map, we'll have to climb down the cliff," Anna said. "There's no other way around."

Olaf peeked over the cliff. "Wow!" His eyes grew wide. Then he laughed. "Let's go!"

Kristoff smiled. "You might want to use a rope! Just go slow and you'll be fine."

Anna smiled and lowered herself over the cliff. "This should be fun!"

"Is Anna going slow enough?" Olaf asked as Anna bounced down the cliff face.

"Well, maybe going slowly isn't as important as going carefully," Kristoff said with a smile.

"I don't think the climbing part is necessary," Elsa said with a sly smile. "I have an easier way."

With a wave of her hand, Elsa used her magic to create an ice slide down the side of the cliff! Then she, Olaf, and Sven slid past Kristoff and Anna. But when the friends got to the bottom of the cliff, they found another cliff to climb up!

After hours of walking along the fjord and climbing up and down hills, the group finally reached the top of Opplading Mountain. To their surprise, nothing was at the summit except bare rocks and large boulders. They looked around, puzzled. Where were the crystals?

The sun was beginning to set, so the group decided to stop for the night. "Maybe we'll have better luck in the morning," Anna said.

The friends set up camp under a rocky overhang. As they settled into their blankets, Kristoff sang a new song he had written. Suddenly, a ribbon of glowing color spread across the night sky.

"I love it when the sky's awake," Olaf said, sighing. "But I've never seen the rocks glow."

Everyone turned to see what Olaf was looking at. Where the light from the colorful sky hit the rocks above them, they could see spots of red, green, yellow, and purple glowing deep inside the boulders!

"Could those be crystals?" Elsa asked.

Kristoff ran his hands over the rock. He took out his climbing ax, but Sven nudged him out of the way.

The reindeer backed up and charged at the rock. His antlers hit it with a loud *BOOM!*

Unfortunately, the sound was more impressive than the tiny cracks that appeared in the rock.

"Maybe I can help," Elsa said. She waved her hand, summoning her powers so that ice formed against the wall and crept into the cracks. The freezing rock forced the cracks wider apart and a small hole appeared.

Seeing her chance, Anna wriggled her hand inside. She didn't get far. "It's too tight," she cried.

"Uh-oh," Elsa said. "The lights in the sky are starting to fade—and the crystals in the rock are, too!"

Anna thought for a moment. "Maybe there's another way. Kristoff, may I see Bulda's crystal?"

Anna reached into the rock again, this time holding Bulda's darkened crystal. As the crystals touched, a magical charge passed between them. Bulda's crystal began to glow again!

The friends cheered. They had restored Bulda's crystal. But as dawn broke, the illuminated crystal began to fade.

"What's happening?" Anna asked.

"I thought we had successfully completed the quest!" Elsa said, shaking her head.

"I guess we had the wrong mountain," Kristoff said.

The friends packed their things and headed back down the mountain toward Arendelle. They were upset that they hadn't been able to recharge Bulda's crystal, but they knew they'd tried their best.

That night, back in Troll Valley, Bulda greeted the group of friends with big hugs.

"We weren't able to recharge your crystal," Kristoff admitted to Bulda. "I'm so sorry."

"Well, this crystal can be finicky," Bulda said with a smile. "Let's take a look."

"Here you go," said Anna. The crystal looked dull and faded in her hands.

The friends gathered together as Bulda held the crystal.

ANNA BOUNCED AROUND THE Arendelle Castle kitchen, placing plates and napkins in a woven basket. She had planned a picnic for her friends and couldn't wait to get started.

"Are you ready?" Elsa asked, peeking into the kitchen.

"Almost. Most of the bags are in the hall, but can you grab that brown one?"

"What's in here?" Elsa asked.

"Just a few picnic essentials," Anna replied.

"You sure you have everything you need?" Kristoff joked. "Maybe you want to bring the stove or perhaps . . . the whole castle?"

"I just want everything to be perfect," Anna said.

"Don't worry, Anna. It'll be great," Elsa said, "because we will all be together."

Anna smiled as she struggled with the bags. "I know, I know, but it doesn't hurt to be prepared."

"Sven and I can help you out with those," Kristoff said, taking them from her.

"Hi, everybody!" Olaf shouted as he ran toward his friends. "Oooh. Is that a real picnic basket? I love picnics. I'm so excited—let's go, let's go, let's go!"

"Let the picnic officially begin," Anna said, leading the way toward the mountains.

As they walked, Anna took a deep breath. "Those spring flowers make the air smell so sweet."

"They really do," said Elsa.

"Mmmmm!" Olaf said as he sniffed a patch of flowers. Olaf had never seen flowers that looked like those before.

He bent down closer and picked a flower.

"Hey, look!" Olaf plucked a petal from the flower and showed it to his friends. "It looks like a heart."

"Wow," Anna said. "I've never seen a flower that shape before. How pretty!"

As they continued up the mountain, something caught Anna's eye. She scooped up a leaf and showed it off. "I found a heart, too!"

Elsa began searching for a heart as well.

"Found one!" she called. Elsa held up a smooth heart-shaped stone.

"I bet I can find one, too," Kristoff said.

"Not before I find another," Anna replied with a grin.

Kristoff found a curved twig and bent it into the shape of a heart. "Got one!" he said. Then the twig snapped in half.

As the friends walked on, they continued to search for hearts. Some things looked like broken hearts. Others looked like perfect hearts. And a few didn't look much like hearts at all.

When they finally arrived at their picnic spot, Kristoff and Anna worked together to surprise everyone.

"Glad I packed those shears," Anna said with a smile.

"Wouldn't be a picnic without them," Kristoff joked.

Setting the shears aside, Anna took out the blanket. "This is the best picnic ever!" Olaf shouted as he helped spread it out.

"Oh, no!" Anna cried as she dug through the picnic basket. She had forgotten to pack the food!

Elsa couldn't believe it. "You packed candlesticks but no food?"

Anna slowly nodded.

Everyone burst out laughing—including Anna.

"Oh . . . but I did remember dessert," Anna said, happily pulling out a
small box and opening it. Anna's smile faded. Her dessert was a melted
mess. "They *were* special chocolates."

Just then, it started to rain. "Oh, come on!" Anna shouted at the sky.

"What a wonderfully refreshing picnic shower!" Olaf said.

The rain came down harder. "Quick! Under the blanket!" Anna said.

The group huddled together, trying to stay dry under the soggy blanket.

"Olaf, it's not supposed to be refreshing when it rains on picnics," Anna said.

"But maybe it should be." Olaf smiled. "The rain is keeping us close. It's like a big cuddly hug!"

Drip. Drip. Drip. The rain started to leak through the blanket and onto their heads.

Anna groaned. This was not the perfect picnic she had pictured. "I'm sorry, everybody," she said. "Should we just forget the picnic and head back to the castle?"

"The picnic's not over," Elsa said. She waved her hands and an ice gazebo appeared.

"Beautiful!" Olaf said.

"And practical," Kristoff added.

"Thanks, Elsa." Anna hugged her sister. "Maybe we can eat the melted chocolate. . . . I'm sure I brought spoons."

Elsa thought for a moment. Then, with a wave of her hands, she magically created an ice mold. "Put the chocolate into this."

It worked! Soon the friends had delicious heart-shaped frozen chocolate treats!

Anna and her friends sat together, eating their treats and watching the rain.

Everyone agreed with Olaf: it was the best picnic ever!

THE PERFECT BIRTHDAY

ANNA WAS EXCITED SINCE the next day was her fifth birthday. That was as many years as she had fingers on one hand! And that made it a very big birthday.

"Oh, I just can't wait!" Anna told her big sister, Elsa, as they got ready for bed. "It feels like it's taking forever for tomorrow to come!"

Just then, Anna and Elsa's mother came to tuck them into bed and say good night.

"You know," Queen Iduna told Anna, "the best way to make tomorrow come faster is to go to sleep. Then, when you wake up, it will be your big day."

Anna smiled as she crawled into bed. "Tell me again what it will be like," she said to her mother.

"Well," Queen Iduna said, "there will be a grand party, with fancy food and beautiful decorations and many important guests. And, of course, a pretty new dress for the birthday girl."

When Anna woke up the next morning, the first thing she saw was her birthday dress sitting in the corner of her room.

"Oooh," she breathed. "It's so fancy!" And it was. With embroidered trim and lace at the hem, it was the prettiest dress Anna had ever seen.

It was perfectly new, perfectly tailored, perfectly . . . perfect!

Anna ate a quick breakfast, and then Gerda helped her into her party dress.

When Anna stepped out of her room, she found Elsa waiting for her. It was time to get their hair done for the party.

"I'll race you there!" Anna cried.

Anna took off running, but she tripped over her own feet and got dust all over herself.

Elsa laughed at her sister and brushed the dress clean. "Come on! We're going to be late!"

Elsa took Anna's hand, and together the two sisters skipped down the hall.

"Birthday curls for the birthday girl!" their hairdresser said when Anna and Elsa arrived. "And braids for her big sister."

The hairdresser set to work. Soon Anna's head was covered with curlers.

"Now don't move," the hairdresser told Anna. "These have to set for one hour."

Anna made a face. How was she going to sit still for a whole hour?

"Want me to read you a story, Anna?" Elsa offered.

"Yes, please!" Anna said. It was hard, but with Elsa's story to focus on, Anna managed to sit still until her hair was finished.

Anna looked in the mirror. Her hair looked perfect! She spun around in a circle. As she did, a single curl came loose. Anna looked at herself again. Now she liked her hair even more!

Soon it was time for
Anna's royal birthday
party. "Wow," she
whispered as she
peeked into the
banquet hall. There
were so many
people!

Anna knew that
perfect manners were
a must at a fancy party.
After all, she didn't want to embarrass
her parents. So with a little wave at Elsa, Anna walked into the hall with
her head held high. She nodded politely at each guest seated at the table.

And when she sat down, she made sure to sweep her skirt under her so
it wouldn't crease.

Anna behaved perfectly all the way through dinner. She kept her elbows off the table, and she made sure to eat everything on her plate. Having perfect manners wasn't exactly fun, but Anna knew her parents would be proud of her.

It was all going great . . . until she let out a loud burp!

"Excuse me!" Anna said, clapping both hands over her mouth. Her cheeks turned red in embarrassment. Burping was *definitely* not perfect manners.

Anna's father smiled. "Don't worry," he reassured Anna. "Sometimes a burp is a compliment to the chef!"

And then the king burped!

"There," he said. "Now the chef knows we *both* enjoyed the meal."

Anna laughed. Her father always knew how to make her feel better.

When the cake came, Anna tried her hardest to eat neatly, but she still ended up with frosting on her face. She crossed her eyes and tried not to giggle at the big, creamy blob on her nose.

But before Anna could do anything, her mother swiped away the frosting . . . and put it right into her own mouth!

"Yum!" she said, winking at Anna.

Anna couldn't help smiling.

That night as she got ready for bed, Anna sighed. She had really been looking forward to her birthday. But she'd been concentrating so hard on acting perfectly that she hadn't had a chance to have much fun!

Suddenly, Anna heard a voice: "Psst!" It was Elsa!

"Are you ready for your real party?" Elsa asked.

"My real party?" Anna responded. "Isn't that what I just had?"

With a grin, Elsa waved her hand. "Royal parties are too proper to be any fun. The best way to celebrate is with a sisters-only party!"

Elsa grabbed Anna by the hand and pulled her into the hall. "There are just two rules," she said. "No manners, and no grown-ups."

Anna and Elsa snuck through the castle as quietly as they could. First the sisters raided the kitchen for leftover birthday cake, which they ate with their hands—no forks or plates!

Then they snuck into the laundry and took out as many pillows and blankets as they could carry. The two dragged their supplies back to their bedroom, where they built the biggest pillow fort Anna had ever seen! The sisters even had a pillow fight.

Just when Anna thought her night couldn't get any better, Elsa gave her a special birthday gift. It was a painting Elsa had made of the two of them. Anna loved it!

Much, much later, Anna and Elsa finally climbed into bed.

"You were right," Anna said. "Sisters-only is way better."

"Did you have a good birthday?" Elsa asked.

"Thanks to you," Anna told her sister, "it was perfect."

ANNA IN CHARGE

THE SUN WAS SHINING bright in Arendelle and everyone was in a good mood. Everyone, that is, except Princess Anna.

"I wish you didn't have to go to the lichen farmers' convention, Elsa," Anna said.

Elsa smiled at her sister. "I won't be gone long, Anna, I promise."

Anna sighed. She knew Elsa would be back the next day, but Anna didn't like to be away from her sister for even a little while.

"Remember, while I'm gone, you're in charge," Elsa said.

"What if I don't know what to do?" Anna asked.

Elsa gave her sister a hug. "Don't worry," she said. "I've written down some tips on how to rule. You'll be fine. And I'll be back before you know it."

In her room, Anna flopped down in her most comfortable chair. She hoped Elsa's note would prepare her for the day ahead.

Just then, there was a knock on the door, and one of the castle guards entered the room.

"Excuse me, Your Highness," the guard said. "You are needed in the throne room."

Anna's heart pounded loudly. There couldn't be a problem already. She hadn't even had time to read Elsa's note!

"Two farmers are having a disagreement," the guard explained. "They are asking for your advice on how to settle it."

Anna followed the guard to the throne room, where the two farmers were shouting at each other. Their voices were so loud that they didn't hear Anna enter.

"Excuse me," she said. But the two men kept yelling.

Anna tried again, but still the farmers didn't hear her.

Finally, the guard whistled sharply. The farmers became silent and turned toward Anna.

"Thank you," Anna said to the guard. "Now what seems to be the problem, gentlemen?"

"His chickens are eating all of my corn!" one farmer shouted.

"Well, his cows keep eating all the grass in my field!" the other farmer yelled back.

Anna listened to the farmers. Each of them thought he was right. How was she supposed to solve their problem? Then she remembered Elsa's note.

Anna opened the note and quickly read the first few lines.

Problems can be hard to solve, Elsa had written. *You have a good heart. Do what you think is right.*

Anna bit her lip. *What do I think is right?* she asked herself silently.

Anna had listened to both sides of the argument. And she had seen that both men had a point. She thought long and hard about what advice to offer. What did her heart tell her was the right thing to do?

Finally, Anna jumped up. "I have an idea," she said. "Let the chickens eat the corn. The cows can eat the grass. And you both can share the milk and eggs!"

Anna held her breath and waited.

The farmers looked at each other. Then they slowly nodded. They both liked that idea!

As the two men walked away arm in arm, Anna smiled. She had solved her first problem of the day!

The farmers had barely left the throne room when Olina came in. She said that the Royal Regatta was about to start, and the Arendelle team was one person short. They might not be able to compete!

Quickly, Anna opened Elsa's note and read the next line. *I hope you aren't bored. Don't be afraid to mix it up!*

How can I mix it up? Anna wondered. Then she had another idea.

Racing down to the water, Anna found Arendelle's team. She jumped into the boat and began to row. When the race was over, Arendelle's boat had come in second place!

Anna was happy that she had helped the team! But her day was just getting started. Next she had a visit with a group of children.

Once again, she pulled out Elsa's note. *You have a great big heart,* Elsa had written. *Use it to have fun.*

Anna thought of all the times she and Elsa had played together when they were children. She realized that she needed to have fun now like she'd had fun *then*!

"Who wants to play hide-and-seek?" Anna shouted.

The rest of Anna's day flew by. She met with the cook to review the menu for the ice harvester dinner the following week. Then she went to see the royal papersmith to make sure the invitations to the annual spring ball were on schedule. She even inspected the troops to make sure their uniforms were spotless.

As the day wound down, Anna went back to the harbor to watch the rest of the boat races and cheer on the other teams.

When the races were finished, she went to the awards ceremony to greet all of Arendelle's guests!

Before Anna realized it, the sun was setting. Plopping down in a chair, Anna let out a huge sigh of relief. *I wonder if this is how Elsa feels at the end of every day,* she thought.

Suddenly, Anna realized that she hadn't finished reading Elsa's note. She opened the scroll. *After a busy day, it is nice to see the stars. The best view is from the roof.*

With the note in her hand, Anna climbed up to the roof. To her surprise, there was a picnic dinner laid out. Next to the food was another note addressed to her.

Excited, Anna began to read. *Good job today,* Elsa had written. *You can be me anytime!*

Anna gasped. She didn't know if she was ready for that!

Looking back down at the note, Anna read the last few lines: *But don't worry. I'll be back tomorrow.*

Anna let out another sigh of relief. Being in charge was a lot of fun, but having Elsa home would be even better!

Disney

FROZEN

BABYSITTING THE TROLL TOTS

ANNA PULLED ON HER boots. Her friends Kristoff and Sven would be there any minute. It was a beautiful spring evening, and they were going to Troll Valley to watch over the toddler trolls while the adults went to their annual magical prophesying convention.

"Are you sure you don't need me to come?" Elsa asked. "I can provide some magical help."

"I think we've got it covered," Anna said, giving her sister a quick hug. "They're just babies.

How hard could it be?"

Soon Anna, Kristoff, and Sven were off toward the setting sun. They admired the dusky sky as Kristoff told Anna stories about growing up with the sweet and silly trolls.

"I wonder if I should have brought games," Anna said. "Do trolls like games?"

"Oh, don't worry," Kristoff responded. "They'll probably sleep the whole time. I bet we'll be relaxing by the fire. Maybe eating some snacks."

He explained that Bulda, his adoptive mother, had a very strict bedtime for all the young trolls.

As soon as they reached Troll Valley, they saw dozens of mossy rocks rolling toward them. Suddenly, the trolls appeared and a chorus of greetings erupted.

"Kristoff! Sven! Anna! Welcome!"

"We missed you!"

"Anna, you're too skinny!" said Bulda. "Let me get some mud pies." Anna politely declined. Then Bulda thanked them for troll-sitting.

Bulda took Anna and Kristoff to the troll tots. "If they get hungry, you can feed them smashed berries. And they may need a leaf change. But it's just about their bedtime, so they should be sleeping soon."

As the adult trolls headed off, Anna waved. "Have a great time! Everything is going to be . . .

"A DISASTER!"

Anna, Kristoff, and Sven had turned to see the toddler trolls had escaped from their pen. They were running, climbing, and swinging all over the place.

"Oh . . . no, no," Anna said, rushing to help a few. "That's dangerous."

Kristoff ran to the leaning tower of trolls that had sprouted.

"All right, guys," Kristoff said, gently pulling the trolls off one another.
"Let's settle down now."

But the more Kristoff, Anna, and Sven tried to calm them, the wilder
they became.

"Maybe they're hungry!" Anna said, heading for the basket of smashed berries.

"Yummy!" she cooed. But the trolls clearly felt they had better things to do.

"Maybe they need changing." Kristoff bravely peered into one of the trolls' diaper leaves. "Nope."

"Let's put them to bed," Anna suggested. "They must be tired by now."

But, alas, the young trolls were wide-awake.

Suddenly, a cheery voice interrupted them.

"Hello, troll babies!"

It was their friend Olaf!

"Elsa sent me in case you needed some help," Olaf explained.

"Boy, are we glad to see you," Kristoff said.

Anna ran to greet the snowman. But in her hurry, she tripped, falling face-first into the basket of berries!

Kristoff rushed to her side. "Anna! Are you okay?"

Anna lifted her head, her face covered in dripping purple goop. The little trolls burst into loud giggles. They stampeded toward her, lapping up the berry juice on her cheeks.

Anna laughed. "Well, I guess that's one way to feed them."

230

After the trolls were done, they sat in a heap, happy and full. Suddenly, a strange smell floated through the air. The trolls looked down at their leaves.

"Uh-oh," Kristoff said. "Olaf, you distract them."

Olaf happily told the little trolls stories about his most favorite thing in the world: summer. Anna and Sven collected leaves while Kristoff changed diapers. Soon everyone was clean and sweet-smelling once more.

"And now for my showstopping song about summer!" Olaf announced.

Anna noticed that the trolls were swaying. Some of them were having trouble keeping their eyes open.

"Actually," she said, "maybe Kristoff and Sven could sing a lullaby."

"Good thing I brought my lute," Kristoff replied while Anna and Olaf put the trolls to bed.

"Rock-a-bye troll-ies, in your small pen. Time to go sleepy for Uncle Sven," Kristoff crooned, changing his voice and pretending to be the reindeer.

By the time the adult trolls returned, the wee ones were sound asleep.

"Wow, great job," Bulda whispered.

"It was easy," Anna replied, elbowing Kristoff.

"Piece of mud pie," Kristoff added.

Bulda hugged her friends. "You two will be great parents someday!"

Elsa's Perfect Plan

QUEEN ELSA SAT IN her study and thought. Her little sister's birthday was coming up, and Elsa couldn't decide how to celebrate it! She wanted to make the day extra special. It had been years since Anna had a real birthday celebration. *I can give Anna a surprise party!* Elsa thought.

The next morning, Elsa consulted with the household servants, Gerda and Kai.

"I'll make sure the silverware is ready and the dishes are washed," Gerda offered.

"And I'll create the menu," Kai said.

"Perfect," Elsa said. "Now I'm free to focus on presents, decorations, and entertainment."

Elsa paced the hall. She knew Anna valued friends and family, but how was Elsa going to turn them into a present?

She glanced up at a huge painting. Suddenly, her face lit up. "I'll give Anna a new family portrait!"

Elsa needed to get to town to begin making arrangements. She turned abruptly and crashed right into Anna!

"Where are you rushing off to?" Anna asked.

"U-um," Elsa stammered. "I was just going to, er, the attic?"

"I can help," Anna said. "What do you need?"

Elsa took a deep breath and blurted out the first thing that popped into her mind. "String! I really need . . . string."

Elsa was worried if she stayed around much longer, she'd ruin the surprise. So she turned and ran—leaving Anna rather perplexed.

With Anna occupied looking for string, Elsa hurried to the village. She knew the bakery had to be her first stop.

"Can you create a huge chocolate birthday cake for my sister?" she asked the baker. "And it needs to be a surprise."

"Of course!" the baker replied. "What kind of chocolate? We have different varieties—"

Just then, Anna burst through the door.

"Elsa!" Anna exclaimed. "I've been looking everywhere for you. I found your string!"

Elsa shot the baker a nervous glance, but the baker had planned many surprise parties. With a wink, he turned to Anna. "Would you like to taste one of our chocolate cupcakes? Or maybe an ice cream cake? Which kind is your favorite?"

After sampling to their hearts' content, Anna and Elsa headed home . . . with just a few extra treats.

Over the following days, Elsa began sneaking into town before Anna awoke. She visited the florist, the jeweler's shop, the children's choir, and even the royal painter.

She wanted everything to be perfect. The big day was almost here! But Anna was feeling lonely. Elsa never seemed to have any time to spend with her.

After so many errands, Elsa was exhausted. That's when Kristoff and Sven walked by. They'd been shopping for a special gift for Anna.

"You look tired," Kristoff said.

"There's no time to be tired," Elsa replied. "I still need to get the decorations."

"Don't worry," he said. "Leave the decorations to Sven and me!"

Meanwhile, Anna was feeling even lonelier. It was odd. She knew it was almost her birthday, but as the day got closer, it seemed as if everyone was ignoring her.

On the evening before her birthday, Anna sighed as she talked with Olaf. "I just want to spend time with Elsa and Kristoff tomorrow. I'd hate for the day to go by without my best friends."

"Why? What's tomorrow?" Olaf asked.

"It's my bir—" Anna paused, then smiled. "It's the summer solstice—a great day to be with friends and family, and do nice things for the people you love."

"What kinds of nice things?" Olaf asked.

"Well," Anna said, "like wash Kristoff's sled! Let's do it!"

It was dusk as Anna and Olaf made their way to the stables, hauling
sponges and a bucket of warm water.

But when they pulled the blanket off the sled to begin their secret task,
there were Kristoff and Sven—asleep!

"What are you doing here?" Kristoff asked, rubbing his eyes.

"I was going to wash your sled," Anna explained. "Kind of a summer solstice surprise."

Kristoff led Anna outside.

"The summer solstice is an important day," he said. "But it's more important because it's your birthday. Do you even know what a real birthday is?"

"Ooh! I know!" Olaf said. "The little trolls told me it's when family and friends get together, and there are candles, and everyone sings and gives presents, and—"

"Yes, songs and presents are nice," Kristoff interrupted. "But they're not what make a real birthday."

Anna sighed. "I may have had that kind of birthday a long time ago, but it's been so long. I don't really remember."

From her bedroom window up high in the castle, Elsa looked out and saw Anna talking to Kristoff.

She opened the window just a crack to listen.

Kristoff cleared his throat. "A birthday is a day when everyone gets to say that they really, really— uh—love—uh, *cake*." Kristoff was blushing.

"Well, I do love cake," Anna said. "That really is a great day!"

Inside the castle, Elsa had just a few more presents to wrap. Then she spotted the string she'd had Anna fetch from the attic. A wonderful idea occurred to her—she would use the string to plan a scavenger hunt throughout the kingdom. It would be a great way to spend the day together!

Just then, there was a light knock at the door. It was Anna. "Um—I can't open the door now," Elsa said. She didn't want Anna to see any of the gifts.

"Elsa?" Anna asked. "You know it's my birthday tomorrow, right?"

"Of course," Elsa said through the closed door. "Would you like to do something together? I've cleared the whole day."

"I'd love that," Anna said.

"Good night, Anna," Elsa said sweetly.

Then she held up the ball of string and smiled. There were only a few hours left until Anna's birthday, and finally Elsa had the perfect plan!

FROZEN

THE ICE GAMES

IT WAS WINTER IN Arendelle—the happiest winter in many years.

Kristoff and Princess Anna were inside, reading quietly in front of a roaring fire. Suddenly, the sound of children's laughter came through the open window. Anna put her book down and went to the window.

"Oh!" she said. "Come look, Kristoff. It's soooo cute!"

Kristoff joined Anna at the window. Three children were building a toboggan in the snowy courtyard below. Kristoff smiled at the children, but Anna could see that he was thinking about something else.

"All right," Anna said. "Out with it. What's on your mind?"

Kristoff turned to Anna. "I didn't have a lot of friends when I was a kid," he said. "I mean, I had Sven. And the trolls. But only humans are allowed to enter the Ice Games."

"The what?" Anna asked.

"Every year on the winter solstice, ice harvesters and their families from all over the world gather on a glacier and hold the Ice Games. It's supposed to be really fun. But you have to have a three-person team." Kristoff looked a little sad. "I bet those kids are building that toboggan for the big race. . . ."

Later, Anna told Elsa what Kristoff had said. "It was so sad to hear him talk about missing the Ice Games," she said. "So I was thinking—"

"That we should take Kristoff to the games this year!" Elsa finished for her, delighted. "The three of us can be a team!"

"Yes!" Anna said, hugging her sister. "I knew you'd get it."

Anna and Elsa quickly packed everything they would need for the journey to the games. Then they ran to tell Kristoff about their plan.

"You'd do that for me?" he asked, his face red.

"Of course!" Anna said. "Every ice harvester should get to go to the Ice Games!"

The day before the winter solstice, Anna, Elsa, and Kristoff arrived at the Ice Games. Anna couldn't help staring at the group around her. She'd never seen so many ice harvesters in one place!

"Say," one of them said, pointing at Elsa, "isn't that the queen of Arendelle? I heard she has magic ice powers."

"No fair!" said another. "She'll use her powers to win the games!"

"I promise on my honor as queen that I will not use my powers in the games," Elsa said.

"Yeah, so back off," said someone with a gruff voice. Anna turned to see a group of ice harvesters from Arendelle standing behind her. With them were the three children she had seen outside the palace window! Anna grinned. She loved that the people of Arendelle were so loyal to her sister.

"Our queen wouldn't cheat," the little girl from Arendelle said. "And she doesn't need to, anyhow."

It was true: Elsa didn't need to use her powers to win the first contest. She carved a gorgeous ice statue of the trolls, using just a hammer and a chisel.

Next was Anna and Kristoff's event.

"I don't care what the event is. I know we're going to win!" Anna said.

"Couples ice-skating," the announcer boomed.

"Unless it's that . . ." Anna said, her heart sinking. She was a terrible ice-skater.

But Anna wasn't one to back down from a challenge. She and Kristoff gave it their all, swooping and speeding around the rink. They didn't win, but they had a lot of fun trying . . . and they did manage to come in third place.

That night Anna, Elsa, and Kristoff had dinner with the rest of the ice harvesters. As they ate, they discussed the Ice Games.

"With Elsa's first-place finish and Kristoff and me coming in third in ice-skating," Anna said, "we actually stand a chance of winning the Ice Games!"

"All we have to do is win the toboggan race tomorrow," Kristoff said.

"Good luck!" said someone in a small voice. Anna turned around to see the little girl from Arendelle.

"Thank you," Anna replied with a smile. "You made the ice sculpture of the palace today, right?"

The girl nodded, blushing furiously.

"It was beautiful," Elsa said. "And I know a little something about making ice palaces!"

Grinning from ear to ear, the little girl ran back to sit with her family.

"Good luck to you, too!" Anna called after her.

"What a sweet little girl," Elsa said. "She reminds me of someone else at her age."

"Me?" Anna asked.

"I said 'sweet,' Anna, not 'annoying,'" Elsa replied with a wink.

Anna punched her sister playfully.

"Of course I meant you, Anna," Elsa admitted.

"One more round of hot chocolate?" Kristoff suggested.

"Yes, please!" Anna and Elsa said together.

As the sun rose the next morning, Anna, Elsa, and Kristoff piled into their toboggan. It was time for the last event.

"Here we gooooooo!" Anna shrieked. The trio rocketed down the slope with the rest of the racers. Anna squinted against the wind as their toboggan went faster and faster. Soon they had pulled ahead of the other racers. "We're winning!" she yelled.

Anna, Elsa, and Kristoff were almost to the finish line when a sled passed them. It was moving so fast they could barely make out who was inside.

It was the children from Arendelle, streaking down the slope and crossing the finish line!

"We won! We won!" the kids yelled, hugging each other and jumping up and down. Watching them celebrate, Anna couldn't bring herself to be disappointed.

She just hoped Kristoff wasn't too upset.

"I'm sorry we didn't come in first, Kristoff," Elsa said later as they took their place on the winners' podium.

Kristoff grinned. "Nah," he said. "Don't be. I finally got to compete in the Ice Games! And I think it's great that they won. Having friends you can count on is really important when you're a kid."

Anna hugged Kristoff. "Having friends you can count on is really important forever. And I have the best friends of all!"

TROLL TREK

PRINCESS ANNA WAS READING a story to the village children. "'That night, the young trolls climbed the highest mountain and grabbed stars out of the sky. They tossed the stars to each other and bounced them off the moon. The dancing lights woke the humans. They gazed at the stars, admiring the display and wondering what was causing it. Suddenly, the lights stopped and everything was still again.'"

Anna sat down to finish the story. "'Back in the Land of Trolls, the troll parents demanded their children put the stars back. And the little trolls obeyed . . . sort of.'"

Delighted, the children clapped their hands.

"Are trolls really real?" a girl named Mari asked.

Anna smiled. "They're not quite like the trolls in the story, but they're real," she said. "Just ask Kristoff."

"How do you know?" a boy asked Kristoff.

Kristoff told them he was raised in Troll Valley. All the children gasped.

"Where's Troll Valley?" Mari asked.

"I can't tell you," said Kristoff. "It's a secret."

The children groaned in disappointment as they collected their things and prepared to leave. But Mari lingered behind.

"Do you mind if I ask you a few questions?" she said to Kristoff. She asked him things like, "Did you grow up by a stream?" and "What types of flowers did you smell during spring?" and "Is it true trolls sleep all day?" Mari wrote down everything he said.

Anna showed Mari where she could find troll books in the royal library. Mari flipped through the books. She wanted to know everything about trolls. But most of all, she wanted to find out for herself if trolls were real.

After hours inside the royal library, Mari headed home with an armful of books.

She stayed up late, reading and trying to separate fact from fiction. When she found an ancient map that mentioned trolls, she studied it and used her notes from her talk with Kristoff to create a map of her own.

The next day, Mari woke up bright and early. She finished her chores as fast as she could, and without saying a word, she grabbed her things and left.

It wasn't long before Mari's parents realized she was gone. They were worried, thinking she was lost. They rushed to the castle. Anna and Elsa immediately gathered others to help search for Mari.

As the villagers set out to look around the kingdom for the lost girl, Anna, Kristoff, and Elsa hurried into the mountains. They were certain Mari had gone in search of the trolls.

"Do you think she'll make it to Troll Valley?" asked Anna.

"I'm not sure," Kristoff said. He suggested they talk to Grand Pabbie. "He'll know what to do."

When they arrived in Troll Valley, Kristoff approached a large boulder that unrolled, revealing Grand Pabbie. "Have you seen a little girl wandering around?" Kristoff asked.

"I have not," said Grand Pabbie. "But Little Rock and I will help you find her."

"You cover the east side of Troll Valley and we'll cover the west," Grand Pabbie said to Kristoff, Anna, and Elsa. "Then we'll meet back here."

And with that, the group split up in search of Mari.

Meanwhile, Mari was walking up the mountain. She stopped beside a twisted, knotty oak tree. When she heard the gentle sound of water, she traced her finger across her map. Kristoff had mentioned a stream. "Aha!" she said.

She followed the water for quite a while before seeing the same knotty tree. "Oh, no," she said. "I just made a circle." She looked up at the setting sun and began to wonder if searching for trolls had been a bad idea.

Mari sat down to examine the map more closely.

As Little Rock and Grand Pabbie crested the hill, they spotted her and stayed out of sight. They had an idea as Mari started off again. They would secretly help her find the way.

They created the landmarks on Mari's map to guide her through the forest. With their help, Mari was on track to reach Troll Valley!

The other trolls joined in and rolled themselves up into boulders, creating the edge of a pathway for Mari.

Soon Anna, Kristoff, and Elsa found her.

"Mari!" Anna called to her. "I'm so glad we found you. Everyone has been so worried."

Mari hung her head. "I'm sorry," she said. "I just wanted to find the trolls."

Mari looked at Kristoff. "So . . . is this where you were raised?"

Suddenly, Kristoff's adoptive mother, Bulda, popped open and blurted out, "Of course it is! He lost his first tooth right over here."

"You *are* real!" Mari gasped. She gave Bulda a hug. When the trolls came out of hiding, Mari knew they had helped her find Troll Valley. "All of you were with me!"

They nodded and smiled. Mari greeted each one and vowed to remember all their names.

That night, after Anna, Elsa, and Kristoff had led Mari back to her grateful parents, Mari decided to create a troll story of her own. Visions of all the wonderful things she could include filled her head as she drifted off to sleep.

ONE EVENING, ANNA AND Elsa's father, King Agnarr, told them a story about the Northuldra, people from an enchanted forest. They had lived in peace with the people of Arendelle, but then everything changed, and the two sides went to war. Angered spirits trapped both groups in the forest, but not before King Agnarr was saved.

After the story, Queen Iduna soothed the girls with a lullaby about Ahtohallan, a special river that was said to hold all the answers to the past.

Many years passed, and though their parents were gone, the girls had found family in their best friends, Kristoff, Sven, and Olaf. But one evening, Anna could tell something was bothering her sister. "You're wearing Mother's scarf. You do that when something's wrong."

Though Elsa refused to admit it, something *was* wrong. Someone—or something—was calling to her.

Later that night, Elsa found herself answering the mysterious voice. As she began using her icy powers, she could feel them changing. They grew stronger and stronger until, finally, she triggered a shock wave that shot across the kingdom. Fire vanished from the torches; the fountains and waterfalls dried up; even the wind died down. Villagers stumbled over the rippling cobblestones and everyone headed for stable ground.

Once the villagers were safe above Arendelle, the ground rumbled once again. Boulders rolled in and popped open, revealing trolls. Grand Pabbie quickly approached the girls. He explained that Elsa had woken the spirits of the Northuldra Forest.

Grand Pabbie told Elsa to follow the voice north. Then he told Anna that she should go along to protect her sister. "I won't leave her side," said Anna.

The sisters, along with Kristoff, Olaf, and Sven, traveled north in search of the forest. But when they found the forest entrance, a wall of mist surrounded it. It wouldn't let Kristoff and Olaf pass through.

But Elsa felt a tug toward the mist. She took Anna's hand and stepped forward, and the mist sparkled and pulled back, providing a path for the whole group.

Once inside the forest, the Wind Spirit, Gale, appeared. It picked them all up and whipped them around and around. Elsa used her magic to protect Anna from a flying branch, and the Wind Spirit took notice. It forced the others out, holding Elsa in its vortex.

Finally, Elsa sent a blast of magic to free herself, and beautiful ice sculptures appeared. Each one captured a different moment in time. Elsa had never created anything like them before!

Olaf reminded them of his theory that ice could reveal the past. "Water has memory," he said.

Soon the trapped Northuldra and Arendellians from Anna and Elsa's old bedtime story appeared. Anna recognized one of the soldiers. It was Lieutenant Mattias, their father's official guard.

The Northuldra noticed that the sisters' scarf was Northuldra. Whoever had saved the king from the forest must have been a Northuldra!

Despite this news, the Northuldra and the Arendellians began to argue until a bright flash of fire appeared. The Fire Spirit dashed around the trees, setting them ablaze. Elsa used her magic to chase it down and discovered the spirit was a small salamander. The voice called, and Elsa and the salamander both turned toward it. The Fire Spirit heard the voice, too! Elsa took this as a sign that she needed to keep going north.

Later that evening, one of the Northuldra explained the symbols on the scarf to Elsa. They represented the four spirits. The Northuldra woman pointed out a fifth spirit, which was called the bridge. Some said they heard it call out the day the mist fell around the forest.

Elsa was now certain that she had to follow the voice she had been hearing in order to set everyone free.

Kristoff and Sven had gone with one of the Northuldra to help with their reindeer, and Elsa refused to wait.

Anna and Olaf joined Elsa, and the three continued north. When they reached the top of a hill, they gasped at the sight below. It was their parents' ship. They realized this meant that their parents had been in search of Ahtohallan when they disappeared. They must have been searching for answers about Elsa's powers.

Elsa vowed to find the mysterious Ahtohallan, even if it meant crossing the dangerous Dark Sea.

Despite Anna's protesting, Elsa had to go alone. She waved her hands, creating a boat, and sent Anna and Olaf sliding down a path of ice. "Elsa, what are you doing? No, no!" cried Anna.

They couldn't stop, and soon they found themselves gliding down a river. Anna noticed Earth Giants sleeping on the shore. Using a branch, she directed their boat away from the Earth Giants.

When Elsa reached the Dark Sea, she stood on the shore. Ferocious waves rose and crashed before her.

She sprinted out onto the water, creating frozen snowflakes at her feet. But the strength of the waves quickly knocked her down. Elsa clawed her way to the surface and climbed a giant rock. She took a breath and dove in.

The Water Nokk, an enormous horse, emerged and began tossing her around.
Elsa created an ice bridle and swung onto its back. At first it bucked, trying
to throw her off, but before long the two were riding through the mountainous
waves to the far shore together.

Back on the river, the current carried Anna and Olaf's boat over a waterfall. It delivered them to a dark cavern.

A strong gust of wind carried a swirl of Elsa's magic into the cavern. It was a signal that Elsa had safely crossed the Dark Sea! The magic formed an ice sculpture revealing a memory of the past.

Now Anna knew why the spirits evacuated Arendelle and how to free the forest. Armed with renewed strength and wisdom, she was ready to set things right.

With the Dark Sea behind her, Elsa trudged through terrible winds and snow. When she finally reached Ahtohallan, the mysterious voice quieted. Just as the words of her mother's lullaby had promised, everything became crystal clear. Elsa knew she had followed the right path and was where she was meant to be.

The journey had changed both her and her sister. And together, they could restore peace and mend a broken land.